MY VOICE WILL BE HEARD

MARCIA NICKS

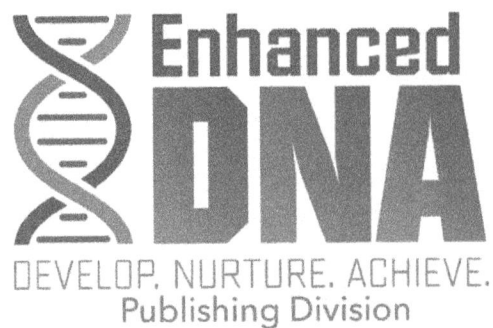

Enhanced DNA Publishing
DenolaBurton@EnhancedDNA1.com
info@EnhancedDNA1.com
317-537-1438

My Voice Will Be Heard
Copyright @ 2022 by Marcia L. Nicks
All rights reserved.

ISBN: 978-1-7378090-3-6
Library of Congress Control Number: 2022918055
Cover Designer: Rose Miller

Dedication

I dedicate this book to my late husband, Comadore Nicks. My love, thank you for being there for me. You inspired me with your wisdom and your calm but stern advice. You stated, "Do not worry about what others think of you, just make sure that you think good of yourself. As long as you do what is right, you will always be pleased with yourself." Thank you, Baby.

I also dedicate this book to my birth mother, Mary Frances Yarbrough Elliott, of whom I named my first-born daughter. I did not have the chance to know you; therefore, I was inspired to write this book to acknowledge to this audience how difficult life can be without your mother.

Acknowlegments

My utmost gratitude is to my Lord and Savior, Jesus Christ. I am grateful for the wisdom that he has given me to complete this book.

I would like to thank my late husband, Comadore Nicks, for patiently listening to me explaining why I should write this book. His final advice was, "Sugar, if you feel this way, I suggest you write the book."

I would like to thank Angela Wynn for inspiring me to stop procrastinating and complete the book. She stated, "You don't have as much time as you think."
I would like to thank my daughter, Dr. Mary Woods, for proofreading and correcting errors in the material. I would like to thank her for helping me to get the book published.

I would like to thank Vincent Burke for also proofreading my material.
I would like to thank my Sunday School class for listening to excerpts and encouraging me to complete the book.

Prologue

My attention has been focused on the many young people that seem to be heartbroken because of broken parental relationships. When your relationship with a parent is compromised, it can cause a child to doubt his or her potential in becoming the best adolescent, preteen, young adult, adult, or individual.

I write this to encourage all who read this book; never give up your dreams, nor allow anyone or anything to impede your ambitions. Your accomplishments are based on your determination and precedence. You can move forward, regardless of the pessimistic challenges that vibrate your surroundings. Everyone has a purpose in life. It is up to each of you to find that purpose and give your best to complete the accomplishment.

I chose this title and subtitle because many times voices are silenced because of circumstances. They are silenced because of shame, low self-esteem, doubt, and a throng of whisperers lying to you. They whisper such things as: you can't, you won't, you are not smart or good enough to be successful. Block the negative vibes and listen to your heart. Your inner voice won't lead you astray.

Table of Contents

Chapter 1: Identifying Your Voice

"If you can speak, just above a whisper; make sure the words spoken are clear."

- Marcia Nicks

Do You Know Your Voice? Probably not!

When this above question is asked, and answered, most people will allude to whether they have the ability to eloquently bellow melodic lovely tunes and melodies, whether the cords are sung in soprano, alto, tenor, or bass. They may conclude that they have a high pitch, low pitch, or deep baritone voice. These are all expressions of the characteristics of a potential voice.

But is this really the voice? Your voice is meant to be heard, understood and reacted to, upon the contents of what was spoken.

In reference to Genesis 1:1, When God began to create the earth; He spoke, and things came into existence. God was not intimidated by the gross darkness nor the voidness of the earth, but he spoke with authority because he knew he was God, and all power was in his hand. You may say, 'I do not have all power!' And yes, you are right. You do not have all power as God does, but you have power to speak and be heard, because you have been given the ability to do so.

Exodus 3:1 Now Moses kept the flock of Jethro his father-in-law, the priest of Midian: and he led the flock to the backside of the desert, and came to the mountain of God, even to Herob.
2 And the angel of the LORD appeared unto him in a flame of fire out of the midst of a bush: and he looked, and, behold, the bush burned with fire, and the bush was not consumed.

The action of the burning bush (**Exodus 3:1-2**) caught Moses' eye. It was not until Moses moved closer, to investigate the bush, that he heard the voice. Here Moses heard an audible voice, the voice of God. Moses was given instruction to lead God's people out of bondage. The voice spoke with a command. In **Exodus 33:18-23**, Moses asked to see **God's Glory.** He hid **Moses in the cleft of a rock until He passed by**. Moses felt his presence and was assured of his blessing.

18And he said, I beseech thee, shew me thy glory.

19And he said, I will make all my goodness pass before thee, and I will proclaim the name of the LORD before thee; and will be gracious to whom I will be gracious, and will shew mercy on whom I will shew mercy.

20And he said, Thou canst not see my face: for there shall no man see me, and live.

21And the LORD said, Behold, there is a place by me, and thou shalt stand upon a rock:

22And it shall come to pass, while my glory passeth by, that I will put thee in a clift of the rock, and will cover thee with my hand while I pass by:

23And I will take away mine hand, and thou shalt see my back parts: but my face shall not be seen.

A Voice, means more than an audible sound that is spoken. Take, for instance, a Deaf person lacks the power of hearing, and a Mute person is unable to speak; however, their voices are heard. Deaf and Mute people use sign language to express themselves.

The great bodies of water do not speak in an audible voice, but they are heard. The swishing and splashing of the water against the rocks and shore. The great sound of the rumbling waves dashing toward us but quietly subsiding the closer it gets to land. Trees do not speak, but you can hear the rustling of the leaves as the wind blows through them. And even the wind, as it blows softly or whirls vehemently, picking up debris in its path. All of these things speak in their own way. What I am trying to convey is there are many ways to be heard. This is the most important concept to embody; that you must be heard.

Self-Exercise 1:

According to The Huffington Post website, there are several steps to finding your voice. In this exercise, list the unique ways that describe your voice. Examine your mind, heart, and soul to identify your passions and what makes you passionate about them. These bullet points of passion will develop your unique voice.

What makes my voice special?

_____

_____

_____

_____

_____

_____

_____

_____

_____

_____

_____

_____

How is it so many people do not know their voice?

According to Webster's Dictionary, the word voice is denoted as 'sound produced through the mouth... as in speaking'. I am not speaking of your physical voice but of your mental capacity to convey what you want known. The synonyms that best describe "Voice Heard" are: express, meaning, to give utterance, or voice of expression.

Your voice does not have to be audible; it is unnecessary to project volume in your voice to be heard. Now, there are times that you will need to speak in an audible voice and to speak loudly. However, you must recognize and understand what to express to be heard in volume. For example, a baby cannot speak. They have to learn how to speak, but if anyone has ever attended to a baby, you would know that God has given them the unique ability to express themselves.

A baby has several cries; however, a mother understands each cry. She knows when her baby is hungry, wet, sleepy, or uncomfortable. Although the baby cannot speak with words, it definitely can communicate its feelings and needs. The baby's cries are their voice.

You may ask the question, "**What is my voice?**" Your voice starts within you. It is that reasoning; that nudge that continues to persuade you to take notice. Once you take note, you ascertain the ability to reason with, and then verbalize the thought. This is when what is being conveyed becomes apparent. However, this is when the entourage of opinions begin.

This is how and when the sound of your voice either speaks loud and clear; or becomes hesitant, soft spoken or silent. Sometimes, your voice can be portrayed in your actions. You may have the tendency to become withdrawn, or allow others to direct your actions or thoughts, causing you to feel worthless or low self-esteem. Some have missed great opportunities because they were afraid to embark on their passions; fearing they will not be good enough. Others have allowed their dreams to become annihilated, because of a setback in the initial debut of your project.

Do not be afraid of setbacks; it is just a chance to step back, observe the problem, improvise or improve the matter, and move forward. Every time you stop because of a situation; you renew the negative thought that you are not qualified to pursue your dream.

To give you a real-life scenario, here is a time I allowed opinions and setbacks to hinder and stop my own progress. My plan was to be a Certified Public Accountant. In my generation, the church had a lot of influence on your career decisions. The focus for new born believers was seeking the presence of God at all cost. While, the ideal Christian belief was great, the understanding of the separation of the natural life and spiritual life was vague to the church.

Christian leaders impressed upon the saints of God that the most important things in life were the spiritual aspects. Therefore, many of the young believers in my day missed great opportunities in seeking a successful career. Instead, I got married and immediately began a family.

My dream was pushed further away.

To this day, I never accomplished my dream. Thankfully, I had enough courage to pursue a degree and received my Bachelor's in Accounting.

Another scenario with a different outcome. Mary (the mother of Jesus) was just a young girl when she became espoused to Joseph. When the Angel appeared to her and told her she was chosen to birth the child, Emmanuel, she believed against all odds. Mary was not intimate with a man; yet, she was impregnated with the Christ child. She was criticized even by Joseph. He decided to break the engagement and took Mary away to avoid a publicize matter. As it was customary, per Hebrew traditions, Mary could have been stoned. There was a peace beyond all understanding; Mary was not afraid or intimidated by what was being said. She knew that God would protect her. As the story continues, the Lord sent an Angel to Joseph commanding him not to break the engagement. The Angel explained that the immaculate conception was by the Holy Spirit. There are no more examples of Mary's experience today. You can hold on to your dreams and be determined to take every step necessary to accomplish that dream.

Self-Exercise 2:

Please answer the following as they relate to your points of passion in Exercise 1.

How does this chapter relate to your points of passion list?

_____

_____

_____

_____

_____

_____

_____

_____

_____

_____

_____

_____

_____

_____

_____

_____

Self-Exercise 2:

Please answer the following as they relate to your points of passion in Exercise 1.
Provide a definition of your understanding of "Your Voice".

_____

_____

_____

_____

_____

_____

_____

_____

_____

_____

_____

_____

_____

_____

_____

_____

Self-Exercise 2:

Please answer the following as they relate to your points of passion in Exercise 1.
List any questions on the material in Chapter 1.

_____

_____

_____

_____

_____

_____

_____

_____

_____

_____

_____

_____

_____

_____

_____

_____

_____

Chapter 2: Has Your Voice Been Silenced?

"Don't let small minds make you doubt and question your abilities. You are more than their negativity."

- Samuel Zulu

We, as humans, are our own worst critics. Your biggest fight is within you. It may terrify you to make a mistake, simply because you have witnessed others become ostracized in their mistakes and actions. Please know that you have the ability to change your outcome by renewing your mind. Romans 12:12, *"Be ye transformed by the renewing of your mind, that ye may prove what is that good, and acceptable, and perfect, will of God"* (KJV).

You are not the person that has been carved for you, neither do you have to react in the manner of those around you. Often parents, mentors, and coaches guide children, learners, and players in a way that is most conducive to a positive outcome. When guidance is produced and received in a positive manner, the outcome is promising. However, when the intent is aggressive, selfish, or even malicious, your voice is minimized and molded into something foreign to you. Do not antagonize yourself. Embrace your unique character and voice.

To give you an example, my father struggled with speaking in public and to individuals. He would often begin to speak at random, rather than staying on course with the subject. When he had to minister before the church, I would sit in my seat and cringe while he was speaking. I would hope that he would properly articulate his words and syntax and stay on course. Although my father could not hear me, I would mumble the word that I knew he was trying to say.

During a one-on-one conversation, my father would either fumble to the actual answer, or he would answer with a lengthy response that many would forget the initial answer. I did not know at the time that my father had a social anxiety disorder; therefore, I did not understand what caused him to react in this manner, as he was an intelligent person.

I do not know if watching him perform in this manner mesmerized me; I feared having to experience this behavior, or if it is hereditary. Unfortunately, I deal with the same problem. Not wanting to inflict the same embarrassment on my loved ones, or to protect my feelings, I chose to remain silent. I now understand that the behavior displayed was an unknown disorder that he could not help.

In **Exodus 4:10,** Moses reckons with the Lord, *"I am slow of speech and cannot speak eloquently"*. God ensured Moses that He would be with Him. To ease Moses' anxiety, the Lord sent Aaron, Moses' brother, with him to speak on Moses' behalf, as Aaron spoke well.

Why?

I do not know what my father experienced while he ministered, but I can share with you my experience. A few days before my speaking engagement, I would begin to have jitters. The day before, I could not eat. My stomach would be churning and my bowels would be loose. Prior to speaking I would hyperventilate, palms would become sweaty, and I felt I was going to upheave everything I ate, which was not much. The moment of presentation my throat would become dry, I felt faint, and my brain skipped town. There I was, fishing for words because the presentation I prepared had escaped.

On multiple occasions, I was told that the performance would improve as I continued speaking. I tormented myself a few times, trying to overcome this monster. Unfortunately, it did not. I decided I could never conqueror this fear. I witnessed others who experienced the same fears. They have gone on to be great orators.

Why?

What was the difference? The difference was mind control and power of the tongue. There are at least two things that can control your destiny and its results: your mind and your tongue. Luke 6:45 stated, *"A good man out of the good treasure of his heart bringeth forth that which is good; and an evil man out of the evil treasure of his heart bringeth forth that which is evil: for of the abundance of the heart his mouth speaketh."* The power of life and death lies within your tongue, (Proverbs 18:21), Be careful of speaking yourself out of or into a result.

Additionally, you cannot take someone else's experience and adopt it as your own. Your voice is not their voice. You have been given a unique voice that is divinely disbursed to you. No matter how well others may perform, you have to find a strategy conducive to your expression. Please let me express that everyone will make a mistake. Do not worry about making a mistake, but impress upon yourself that you do not allow the mistake to overwhelm you to a detrimental state.

Self-Exercise 3:

Spend time with yourself each day – away from all the negativity. Focus on the power you have within you. Each person has the power to make decisions about his or her methods of expressions. The freedom to choose is based on the resources and opportunities by which you may exercise. Identify your support group.

Who can help you develop your voice?

_____

_____

_____

_____

_____

_____

_____

_____

_____

_____

_____

_____

_____

_____

Self-Exercise 3:

What resources do you need to develop your voice?

_____

_____

_____

_____

_____

_____

_____

_____

_____

_____

_____

_____

_____

_____

_____

_____

DO YOU HAVE LOW SELF-ESTEEM? WHY?

Was it because you heard over and over again you were nothing and that you would never be anything? Just like using White-Out to erase mistakes, imagine using the same technique to negate all negative words spoken to you and about you. Wipe it all clean.

The Lord has ordered your steps from the beginning of your conception. He has created you in His image, and everything He has made is good. What others say or how they make you feel is not ordained for you. Push beyond the negative energy to find your potential.

There was a television series I used to watch years ago. I do not remember the name of the show, but the plot of the movie was how and what these individuals did to solve problems. The following is the objective of the movie:

> The characters that were trying to stop or prevent a disaster had to go through this whirl wind to go into another time zone or dimension in order to view the situation from a different perspective. Once they realized the problem and devised a plan, they had to reenter the whirl wind and implement the plan.

There is no tangible whirl wind or matriculating portals, but you can invent a mental whirl wind that will enable you to see the correct perspective of your purpose. It is not relevant what someone thinks or speak about you, but it is relevant what you think or say, (Proverbs 18:21) "There is life and death in the power of the tongue." Your mind is a powerful tool; you can become, what you continue to verbalize. Do not speak out of frustration or anger.

Always think about what it is you want to convey to yourself first, then to others. There are times when a message can be loud and clear without a verbal expression.

Self-Exercise 4:

Cultivate your ability to examine the world around you. What angers you? What motivates you? Can you focus more on your talents? Chapter Two encourages you to renew your mind and make a change that is best for you. Please answer the following questions.

Can you envision a different path to take to avoid the silencing of your voice? Explain?

_____

_____

_____

_____

_____

_____

_____

_____

_____

_____

_____

_____

Self-Exercise 4:

How will you implement the renewing of your mind?

_____

_____

_____

_____

_____

_____

_____

_____

_____

_____

_____

_____

_____

_____

_____

_____

Self-Exercise 4:

In what areas do you agree or disagree with Chapter Two? Explain.

_____

_____

_____

_____

_____

_____

_____

_____

_____

_____

_____

_____

_____

_____

_____

Chapter 3: Watch That Silent Treatment

"First they ignore you
Then they laugh at you.
Then they fight you.
Then you win."

- Unknown

Not all silent treatments are realized or intentional. However, some silent treatments are used to transfer a sense of self-worthlessness. My birth mother passed away when I was three. I can't remember being told "I **love you**". I was never **hugged** or given any form of affection that a child desperately needs to help them be developed and function in everyday life. **Now was I loved? Sure!** A child needs that assurance that he or she is loved. Many parents' goals are to succeed and have financial stability, and there is nothing wrong with that desire. Ask a child that is showered with numerous gifts, yet rarely sees their parents if they felt they were loved; more than likely their answer would be, 'No'.

A child's ultimate satisfaction is to experience the maternal and paternal affection of their parents' physical love. Parents have to work, understandably. I am not against that, but there has to be a balance, because a child needs their parent's participation in their life. If you have a parent that cannot see your potential, or if you have a parent that goes out of their way to make your life miserable; do *not* blame yourself.

It hurts, many tears are shed, and you ponder the thought, 'what did I do?'. Do not withdraw or hold back your potential. It is not your fault. As a matter of fact, take that negative energy and turn it into positive energy. Catapult yourself to your desired direction.

In Genesis 50:20, Joseph told his brothers, *"But as for you, ye thought evil against me; but God meant it unto good, to bring to pass, as it is this day, to save much people alive."* Meaning, many may conspire evil against (mean it for your bad), but God used it for my good. Do not worry about what others say or do. You will hurt, but do not be discouraged. Do not give up. By the help of the Lord, you will accomplish what you aim your mind to do.

Self-Exercise 5:

Do you feel your voice developing? Can you view yourself with a voice from a different perspective?

Write one to two paragraphs describing yourself with a voice in the third person. Write your character as bold and vivacious as you want to be. After you finish writing, ask yourself if you can speak from this character's voice in your life.

_____

_____

_____

_____

_____

_____

_____

_____

_____

_____

_____

_____

DO YOU FIND YOURSELF ALWAYS STEPPING BACK AND LETTING OTHERS GO BEFORE YOU?

Is it because you have little confidence in yourself? Is it that I am not good enough, not as pretty as others, my skin tone is different, I am too short, too tall, too thin, too big, I have short hair, etc.? Do not be bothered with these minute characteristic differences. To be honest, no one is totally satisfied with themselves; we often judge ourselves. If you cannot speak well, but have great penmanship, my advice is to use your penmanship as your voice. God has given you that gift. If your gift is in sports, music, arts, or service of diverse capacities do what is gifted to you and make it one hundred percent.

Never compare yourself to anyone. You may seek someone to be a mentor or as an inspirational guide, however, do not judge yourself. When I was young ,and even sometimes in the present time, I would step back and let others go before me. This was a trained behavior. I was not made or told to step back; this was because of those silent actions I spoke of earlier. Previously mentioned, my mother passed when I was a toddler. I was then placed in a situation of having a stepmom and siblings. When a child loses that maternal protection, it is like you are always caught in the net of deceptive circumstances. I resorted to survival skills as a child, doing whatever was necessary to not be noticed.

My resolution was to stay in my room while others were out laughing, playing, and enjoying life. On top of that, I developed a sensitive complex because of my dark skin complexion. It seemed that the fair-skinned individuals always had the straight long hair, and it was portrayed that they were prettier.

They were always chosen first, and I was in the group that was chosen second or last. Yes, I experienced these things mentioned. I am telling you that you can move past these hinderances.

I heard someone state they told their daughters, "**Every morning go to the mirror and speak this to yourself. I am beautiful, intelligent, God-fearing, and I can do all that I put my mind to do by the help of the Lord.**" I am asking you to apply this same technique in your life. This will increase your confidence and give you a new zeal to press forward. But let me leave you with this token of advice. **Genesis 1:31**, is written as such, *"And God saw every thing that he had made, and behold, it was very good..."* Whether your complexion is fair or dark, you are beautiful.

How long has your voice been silenced?

Some may say that my voice has been silenced too long for me to count. Others may know exactly when that occurrence begin, and yet others may have no clue when it started. That is alright. The most important thing now is to break the silence.

Yes, I know it may not happen all at once, but we must work on it daily. Do not try to do what was meant for others. Only do what you can accomplish and do it well. Stop listening to what others think you should do. Do what makes you happy, as long as it is legal and just. Stop waiting on others to praise you; sing your praise by doing **You. Remember**, it is not what others think of you; rather, what **you think** of yourself. Do not wait for the world to change; change yourself.

Self-Exercise 6:

By now, you should have the confidence to share your voice.

**What is it that you want to say? Are you still holding back?
If so, explain why?**

_____

_____

_____

_____

_____

_____

_____

_____

_____

_____

_____

_____

_____

_____

Chapter 4: You Are Not Alone

"God hears and He sees, and you are not alone in your struggles. Remain firm and stable, for God has your deliverance planned."

\- Joyce Meyer

Many times in life, incidents occur that are beyond our comprehension and control. When incidents such as these seem to occur more often than usual, you begin to blame yourself. Often, these phrases are stated by those who feel abandoned or lost:

"There is no way this can continue to happen if I am doing what I should."

"What is wrong with me?"

"Why do these things happen?"

"I am not as good as others; is this why this happened?"

These are examples of thoughts that may plague your mind. I want to encourage the many victims that experience these occurrences. Although we cannot stop or hinder such incidents, I can attempt to nurse the wounds that often leave a nasty scar. But first, I must express to all this is not your fault. There is nothing you have done to cause these experiences. I want to make you aware that you are not alone.

I recall an incident when I was three years old. Many times, I would stay with a lady that was not my mother. Years later, I found out that she was not my mother, after I was older and inquired of her. I was told that I stayed with this lady very frequently, without any explanation. This disturbed me, because I cannot remember my mother.

I am sure it was for a good reason; however, it gave me a sense of separation. I felt isolated and alone, therefore I became withdrawn and stayed to myself. I thought I was doing the right thing because it was easier than going out to mingle with others. I did not know if I would be accepted or rejected. (After all, there had to be a "negative" reason why I could not stay with my mother and family). Normally, everyone wants to feel the warm embrace of their mother. Yet, I was taken from my mother to stay with someone else. Don't get me wrong; I do not recall any negative encounters with this lady. I just remember being alone with her.

After moving to a new house with my dad, stepmother, and siblings, the incidents became more difficult. I was involuntarily isolated even more. I was sent to my room numerous times. These reasons were not related to mischievous or ill-mannered behaviors. I did not speak out of turn; I was secluded simply because my presence was not pleasing. I was spitefully picked on by a few siblings. Many of my belongings were purposely destroyed by a younger sibling without any consequences. If I complained about the situation, I was told not to cause any conflict. I was made to feel that I was the problem, as many times I was promptly told there was peace while I was gone.

My brother and I, who shared biological parents, would spend the summer and other vacations with our maternal grandmother. While we were gone, our personal belongings were destroyed. I was made to feel like an intruder in my own home. It was my oldest sister who provided parental care for me. She was the one I would talk to about my problems.

While my story includes detrimental occurrences from a step-parent and siblings, there are many that may have similar negative interferences with their biological parents, siblings, or relatives. I am sure others have stories like mine or something different. It does not matter the story, the outcome still affects you in a negative way. You may feel that nothing you do is right, your very best is not good enough, and all that you do receives little to no recognition.

> Genesis 5:2, Male and female created he them; and blessed them, and called their name Adam, in the day when they were created.

Your goal may be to please your parents; instead, they are displeased. In your mind, you may think, "What more can I do?" Let me help you to understand. You were created in the image of Jesus (Genesis 5:2, KJV).

> Genesis 1:31, And God saw every thing that he had made, and, behold, it was very good. And the evening and the morning were the sixth day.

Everything He made was very good (**Genesis 1:31, KJV**). You must remember that you do not need anyone's approval to feel accepted. When you were born, you were good. Only one rule you should have, and that is, do your best in all that you do. It is not up to anyone else to make you happy. **You** must put forth the effort to make you happy. **You** accomplish your goals. It will not always be easy, but it will be rewarding. Do not give up your dreams because those surrounding you are not in agreement with your decision. As long as your decision is for the betterment of your status and not harmful to you or to others; then go for it and accomplish your best.

My encouragement is to give you confidence in accomplishing those positive goals you have set for yourself. I want you to understand that even though there is opposition, you can still achieve your goals. This is not a get out-of-jail card, rather, this is an uplifting card. You must be obedient to your parents, teachers, coaches, and whomever is in leadership over you.

Remember, Jesus was born as a baby. Growing up, He had to be obedient to his parents until the time of his mission began. Jesus is a great example for us all. I am sure there were decisions that the parents made that could have been debated, simply because He knew the right decision; however, Jesus humbled himself, and preformed as a child.

While persevering to achieve your goals, remember, the best way to do that is with a kind spirit, humble heart, willingness to listen, eagerness to learn, and with an understanding that there may be difficulties. Always remember this proverb: 'Having or accomplishing anything good is worth fighting for'.

Self-Exercise 7:

The final step in developing your voice is to find your strength in someone who believes in you. The person can be a mentor, coach, teacher, or family member.

If you had the ultimate support, how would you make your voice speak volumes? Explain. Not only explain, but go forth and be who you are created to be.

_____

_____

_____

_____

_____

_____

_____

_____

_____

_____

_____

_____

_____

Self-Exercise 7:

How did this book and the discussions help you?

_____

_____

_____

_____

_____

_____

_____

_____

_____

_____

_____

_____

_____

_____

_____

_____

I hope this message was helpful and relatable, as it was my intention to uplift and encourage you. In all things give praise to God and He will go with you. May God be with you and bless your every step. Go with God and He will go with you.

The End of the book, but the beginning of a NEW you!

References

Caldwell, C. (2020). Motivation and identity – Finding your voice. INTERNATIONAL JOURNAL OF MULTIDISCIPLINARY RESEARCH AND ANALYSIS. 3(03), 1-8. Retrieved from 1.pdf (ijmra.in)

Davidji's Blog. (2022). 7-Steps to finding your voice. Retrieved from 7 Steps to Finding Your Voice – davidji

The Huffpost Wellness. (2022). 7-Steps to finding your voice. Retrieved from 7 Steps to Finding Your Voice | HuffPost Life

About the Author

Marcia Nicks is an Indianapolis, Indiana native. She was born into a family of 17 siblings and is the mother to nine children, 29 grandchildren and ten great-grandchildren. Her lineage stems from a branch of pastors and preachers. Her grandmother, Jennie Yarbrough-Forster, was the founder and pastor of the Believers in Christ Tabernacle Church in Indianapolis, Indiana. Upon the passing of her grandmother, Marcia's father, Palo Stewart Elliott, pastored the church.

Marcia exercises two gifts of the spirit: giving and teaching. She was a Sunday School Teacher for ages 10-12; a youth leader for camps and excursions; and the leader of the youth choir. Additionally, Marcia became the director of plays performed at Believers in Christ, many of those plays she wrote. Marcia knows all too well the pain caused by her muted voice; ergo, she was inspired to write this book as a legacy to her family and to those who are struggling with a muted voice.

Be Encouraged,

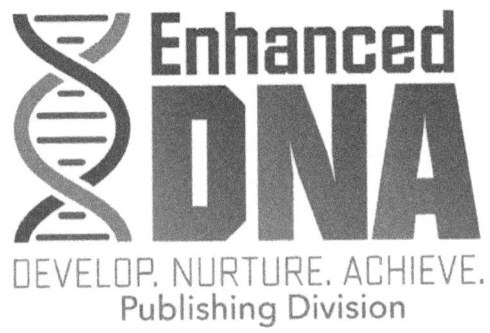